KEYBOARD PERCUSSION

HOLIDAY FAVORITES

Solos and Band Arrangements
Correlated with Essential Elements® Band Method

Arranged by ROBERT LONGFIELD, JOHNNIE V...
MICHAEL SWEENEY and PAUL LAVENDE...

T0081640

Welcome to Essential Elements Holiday Favorites! There are two versions of each selection in this versatile book. The SOLO version appears in the beginning of each student book. The FULL BAND arrangement of each song follows. The ONLINE RECORDINGS or PIANO ACCOMPANIMENT BOOK may be used as an accompaniment for solo performance. Use these recordings when playing solos for friends and family.

PLAYBACK+
Speed • Pitch • Balance • Loop

To access audio visit:
www.halleonard.com/mylibrary

Enter Code
1954-8116-4474-2158

ISBN 978-1-5400-2802-0

Copyright © 2018 by HAL LEONARD LLC
International Copyright Secured   All Rights Reserved

00870020

Visit Hal Leonard Online at
www.halleonard.com

Contact Us:
Hal Leonard
7777 West Bluemound Road
Milwaukee, WI 53213
Email: info@halleonard.com

In Europe contact:
Hal Leonard Europe Limited
42 Wigmore Street
Marylebone, London, W1U 2RN
Email: info@halleonardeurope.com

In Australia contact:
Hal Leonard Australia Pty. Ltd.
4 Lentara Court
Cheltenham, Victoria, 3192 Australia
Email: info@halleonard.com.au

AULD LANG SYNE

KEYBOARD PERCUSSION
Solo

Words by ROBERT BURNS
Traditional Scottish Melody
Arranged by MICHAEL SWEENEY

FELIZ NAVIDAD

KEYBOARD PERCUSSION
Solo

Music and Lyrics by
JOSÉ FELICIANO
Arranged by PAUL LAVENDER

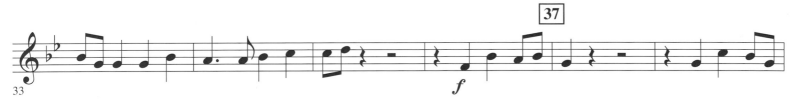

00870020

PARADE OF THE WOODEN SOLDIERS

KEYBOARD PERCUSSION
Solo

English Lyrics by BALLARD MacDONALD
Music by LEON JESSEL
Arranged by PAUL LAVENDER

Toy March

GOOD KING WENCESLAS

KEYBOARD PERCUSSION
Solo

Words by JOHN M. NEALE
Music from PIAE CANTIONES
Arranged by ROBERT LONGFIELD

00870020

PAT-A-PAN
(Willie, Take Your Little Drum)

KEYBOARD PERCUSSION
Solo

**Words and Music by
BERNARD de la MONNOYE**
Arranged by ROBERT LONGFIELD

Silver Bell

KEYBOARD PERCUSSION
Solo

**Words and Music by
JAY LIVINGSTON and RAY EVANS**
Arranged by PAUL LAVENDER

00870020

DO YOU HEAR WHAT I HEAR

KEYBOARD PERCUSSION
Solo

Words and Music by
NOEL REGNEY and GLORIA SHAYNE
Arranged by MICHAEL SWEENEY

Moderately

rit.

00870020

From THE SOUND OF MUSIC

MY FAVORITE THINGS

KEYBOARD PERCUSSION
Solo

Lyrics by OSCAR HAMMERSTEIN II
Music by RICHARD RODGERS
Arranged by ROBERT LONGFIELD

From the Motion Picture Irving Berlin's HOLIDAY INN

WHITE CHRISTMAS

KEYBOARD PERCUSSION
Solo

**Words and Music by
IRVING BERLIN**
Arranged by JOHNNIE VINSON

00870020

CHRISTMAS TIME IS HERE

KEYBOARD PERCUSSION
Solo

Words by LEE MENDELSON
Music by VINCE GUARALDI
Arranged by JOHNNIE VINSON

00870020

From Warner Bros. Pictures' THE POLAR EXPRESS

KEYBOARD PERCUSSION
Solo

Words and Music by
GLEN BALLARD and ALAN SILVESTRI
Arranged by JOHNNIE VINSON

AULD LANG SYNE

KEYBOARD PERCUSSION
Band Arrangement

Words by ROBERT BURNS
Traditional Scottish Melody
Arranged by MICHAEL SWEENEY

00870020

FELIZ NAVIDAD

KEYBOARD PERCUSSION
Band Arrangement

Music and Lyrics by
JOSÉ FELICIANO
Arranged by PAUL LAVENDER

00870020

PARADE OF THE WOODEN SOLDIERS

KEYBOARD PERCUSSION
Band Arrangement

English Lyrics by BALLARD MacDONALD
Music by LEON JESSEL
Arranged by PAUL LAVENDER

00870020

GOOD KING WENCESLAS

KEYBOARD PERCUSSION
Band Arrangement

Words by JOHN M. NEALE
Music from PIAE CANTIONES
Arranged by ROBERT LONGFIELD

00870020

PAT-A-PAN
(Willie, Take Your Little Drum)

KEYBOARD PERCUSSION
Band Arrangement

Words and Music by
BERNARD de la MONNOYE
Arranged by ROBERT LONGFIELD

00870020

SILVER BELLS

KEYBOARD PERCUSSION
Band Arrangement

Words and Music by
JAY LIVINGSTON and **RAY EVANS**
Arranged by PAUL LAVENDER

Easy Feel

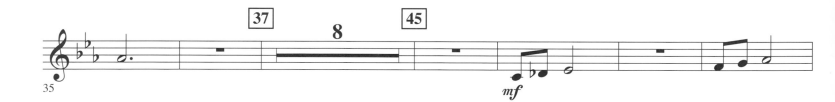

00870020

DO YOU HEAR WHAT I HEAR

KEYBOARD PERCUSSION
Band Arrangement

Words and Music by
NOEL REGNEY and **GLORIA SHAYNE**
Arranged by MICHAEL SWEENEY

Moderately

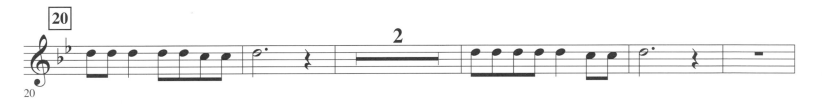

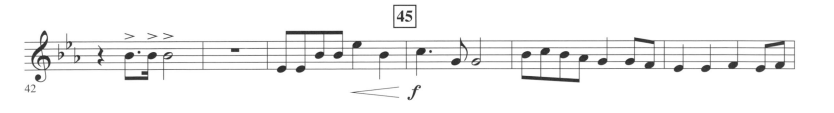

00870020

From THE SOUND OF MUSIC
MY FAVORITE THINGS

KEYBOARD PERCUSSION
Band Arrangement

Lyrics by OSCAR HAMMERSTEIN II
Music by RICHARD RODGERS
Arranged by ROBERT LONGFIELD

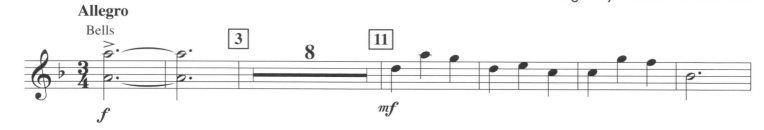

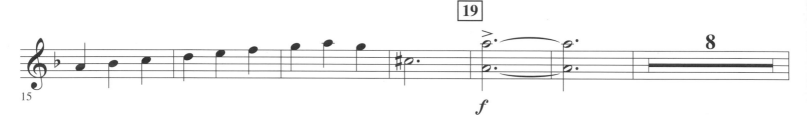

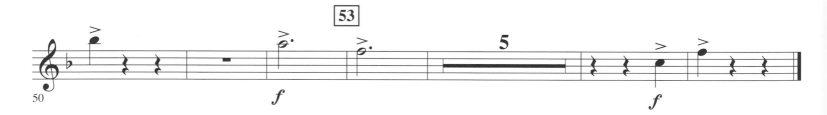

From the Motion Picture Irving Berlin's HOLIDAY INN

WHITE CHRISTMAS

KEYBOARD PERCUSSION
Band Arrangement

Words and Music by
IRVING BERLIN
Arranged by JOHNNIE VINSON

Moderate Tempo
Bells (opt. Chimes)

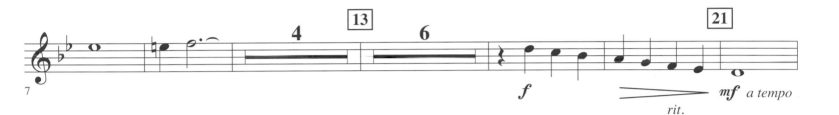

CHRISTMAS TIME IS HERE

KEYBOARD PERCUSSION
Band Arrangement

Words by LEE MENDELSON
Music by VINCE GUARALDI
Arranged by JOHNNIE VINSON

Moderately Slow, Smoothly

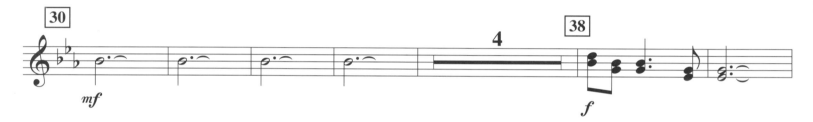

From Warner Bros. Pictures' THE POLAR EXPRESS

THE POLAR EXPRESS

KEYBOARD PERCUSSION
Band Arrangement

Words and Music by
GLEN BALLARD and **ALAN SILVESTRI**
Arranged by JOHNNIE VINSON

Moderately Fast

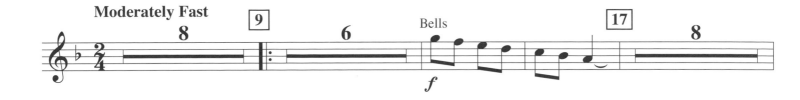